Where You Were

Stephanie Constant

Where You Were © 2022 Stephanie Constant

All rights reserved.

No part of this publication may be reproduced, stored in a retrieval system, or transmitted, in any form or by any means, electronic, mechanical, photocopying, recording or otherwise, without the prior written permission of the presenters.

Stephanie Constant asserts the moral right to be identified as author of this work.

Presentation by *BookLeaf Publishing*

Web: www.bookleafpub.com

E-mail: info@bookleafpub.com

ISBN: 9789357619202

First edition 2022

It's Complicated

"It's Complicated" cannot even begin to explain
This thing we have become
Your scent is still sweet honey
That begs my heart to hum
Though it is shattered glass

You say you've always loved me
You just wanted something more
Than my everything I gave you
And so you slammed the door
Leaving only shattered glass

Stars

We used to lay beneath the stars.
I would tell you their names and their stories.
You would hold me close
Smelling of campfires and cloves.

Now I must explore the universe outside of you
And slowly return to the stars
Dancing just out of reach

What Could Have Been

Some days I am strong.
I hold my head up
And no longer long
For the what could have been.

Some days I am not.
But I must pretend
To not care a lot
For the what could have been.

Where You Were

It's not that you're gone,
it's the loss of what could have been.

The smiles
The little moments
Everything we used to share

I look over to where you were
And I hate you for leaving.

If

5

I try not to think
If maybe I had been more,
If I had been stronger,
If I had more ardor,
If I dressed differently,
If I made time to explore,
If I gave up on my dreams,
If I spoke with candor,
Maybe you would have stayed.

Grief

The sycamore stands naked,
Unabashed in its frozen glory.
I reach out to join the branches
Grasping at the clear blue sky.

Hope

Hope is the tiniest whisper in the midst of the cacophony. It doesn't say it will be ok, but assures that you will survive.

Will Be

I pray that you will be
Everything that I could not -
That you will keep your voice
And fight what must be fought;

That you will know your way
Without sorrow or despair;
That you will never have to feel
The burdens that I bear;

That you will find joy
And love that never ends;
That you will know yourself
And easily make friends;

That you'll find for every question
The answers that you sought;
And you grow up to become
The person I could not.

In the Middle of the Night

It is three A.M.
And once again
My baby clings
To the comfort I bring
In the middle of the night.

She is heavy, dozing,
Face gently nosing
Into my shoulder
As I hold her
In the middle of the night.

I cannot say I mind
That she is still inclined
To wake for a snuggle
Or maybe a couple
In the middle of the night.

Years later I know I
Will miss this time gone by
When she calls out "Mommy, hug!"
And is my snuggle bug
In the middle of the night.

I Was Going to Clean Today

I was going to clean today.

But then there was an email
And a wrong number text,
A dirty diaper,
Remembering that next
Tuesday there's a meeting
On my unfinished project,
Dinner to be made,
And snuggles with a perfect
Daughter who again
Feels she must object
To the folded laundry
Collecting to be yet
Put away.

I was going to clean today,
But maybe I'll just rest.

Toddlers

Pumpkins, peas,
Carrots, cream cheese,
Pancakes, pasta,
Soybeans, salsa,
Brisket, brie,
All you will eat -

But heaven forbid chicken nuggets.

I Never Thought

Rules I never thought I'd need to make:

1) No Wiggles before daybreak
2) Don't high-five Mom in the face
3) Don't try to climb the fireplace
4) We do not eat the puppy's food
5) Please don't run while you are nude
6) Cotton swabs are not for noses
7) Do not stand on garden hoses
8) Don't hit the window with your dolls
9) Milk is not for painting walls
10) Do not wear your dinner plate

…these are all rules I've had to make.

The Playground

Her tiny hands grab mine,
Pulling me to make sure I come
To see her play
To see her run
As fast as she can in the afternoon sun.

Wonder

Eyes take in all anew
Reveling in the wonder
Of the blue sky,
The grasses,
The leaves.

You say "Wow!"
From the depths of your little heart
And there is nothing that could say it better.

Bubbles

Bubbles floating
Pop!
Chasing, laughing
Pop!
Sunlight dancing
Pop!
Fingers reaching
Pop!
Noses wrinkle
Pop!
Eyes twinkle
Pop!
Pop!
Pop!

Baking Cookies

Specks of flour in daffodil hair,
Chocolaty lips beaming bright,
Mixing bowls and Tupperware
Stool to stand at counter height.

Hygge

Tea in hand
Curtains drawn
Daughter napping
Music on
Book open
Snuggled warm
Candle flickers
Thunderstorm

To Be a Leaf

Oh to be a leaf
Falling, letting go
Letting come what may
And landing where I should be.

Fly Away

If the ocean became the sky
Do you think I
Could float away
And see the sky again

www.ingramcontent.com/pod-product-compliance
Lightning Source LLC
LaVergne TN
LVHW050313200726

843509LV00015B/3301